SNOW WATER COVE

JEANNINE SAVARD

SNOW
WATER
COVE

CARNEGIE MELLON UNIVERSITY PRESS   PITTSBURGH   2006

Library of Congress Control Number: 2005933964
ISBN-13: 978-0-88748-455-1
ISBN-10: 0-88748-455-7
Copyright © 1988 by Jeannine Savard
All rights reserved
Printed and bound in the United States of America

See Acknowledgments, page 64, for permission statements.

First Carnegie Mellon University Press Edition, 2006

10 9 8 7 6 5 4 3 2 1

Snow Water Cove was first published in 1988 by the University
of Utah Press.

The publisher expresses gratitude to James Reiss and
James W. Hall for their contributions to the
Classic Contemporaries Series.

CONTENTS

I. *Sermon on the Lake*

II. *White Horizon*

III. *In the Open Air*

I

SERMON ON THE LAKE

Forgetting someone is like
Forgetting to put out the light in the back yard
And leaving it on all day . . .

— Amichai

. . . deep inside me
Where forgetfulness and memory make their deals.

— Transtromer

THE BIRTH OF THE MORTICIAN'S GODDAUGHTER

Afraid to visit, refusing to enter
By the front door with the rest, I
Took the narrow path
Around the lace mill. Men, just off
Their shift from the dye room, pulled
Pink, black, and sea-green swatches
From their sleeves. I've seen
Their daughters on the millhouse porches,
Each of them with a doll
Swaddled in their fathers' mistakes,
And always the dolls were dancing.

On the other side of the white garage
The waxed hearse was new and shimmering
In the June heat, gladiolas
Wilting in their tired wicker baskets,
And the screen door open, forgotten,
Letting in the newly hatched
Black flies. I followed them
And stopped in the foyer . . . Ten minutes more

And I would have been born here: My mother
Was wearing white stockings that night
Upstairs where she and my father were the life
Of the party, dancing and singing
And all that satin down below, mauve pillows,
And gray heads resting
Beside the pinched-out candles. She
Erased it all from her mind,
She said, that was a time to be happy. As strong

As my godfather's after-shave, a cool breeze
Came up from the ramp that led to the
Once-forbidden cellar. Still standing there,
I heard my mother's voice call down to me:

Is it you? We've all been waiting.

[3]

A MILL TOWN IN LATE AUTUMN

Under the streetlights, boys
Just out of the showers are nearing
The perfect face of a woman
They won't see: Her white hair,
Breasts that pull at the spine,
And eyes wrinkled around a dry silence . . .
                    All the buses are late
But she'll wait under the open window,
Under the clicks and whirrs of the sewing machines
Of the second shift. She'll
Remember him, ten years ago, in a gray coat
Drunk on her step making promises
To the door he thinks is her
If just once more
                    she'll let him
Be hidden, carried down into the oil
Of the lamp and without a word.

THE FLORIST'S WIDOW

First, she stopped dressing herself
In the morning, and then, eventually
She slept until the noon delivery
Was set on her doorstep. A bottle of wine
Every day for months kept her
As she watched the vapors rise
Clinging to the glass roofs
Of the greenhouses. The poinsettias

That had not sold were shrinking
But their yellow clustering eyes
Continued to expand, holding her
To blame. Even as she sipped to their health,
Clicking her tongue to the roof of her mouth,
She knew they would be pulled
From their pots and flung
To the leafpile beside the fertilizer shed.
There they would be forgotten

Until the children, in spring,
Would steal themselves out
Of their rooms at night and meet there
With tin cans and flashlights for night crawlers.
Years ago, her husband would wake
To them, tipping
In the dark as he fumbled with his robe
And cursed his way across the yard,
The children's laughter
Down the open street
Like loosening bales of burning straw.

She always dreamed those nights
That the great open jawbone of the lily
Would shut down around her neck
And she would be swallowed
By its narrow stem, settling in the soil
While all the mothers in the neighborhood
Would praise this monster
For its strength and beauty. She would wake

And plead with her husband to leave
The children alone in the future . . . First

It's worms, he said, then the empty flats
Torn apart and nailed to trees for spyhouses,
Then, the devil knows what . . .
                              She'd sip another glass.

OCTOBER NIGHTS

The night before the church fire
He thought he heard a tocsin
Sounding up the throat and through
The belfry walls, bells gutting
The streets, and a wind-suck horse
Jerking back, just short
Of the dizzying gorge. I knocked

And your father answered, his body
Swept behind the opening door,
His head straining to his left shoulder
While the lights
From the highway flashed in his eyes
Like the heads of nails just struck. You

And your mother in your burnoose
Bathrobes in a hotel for the week
And he, he was "sweating it out." No booze

For days.
But Martha, you should know,
He had made friends
With the young skunk from the cemetery.
His Junior Engineer, black with white stripes —

He said it this way —
A moonwalk over New York.

SIX O'CLOCK IN NOVA SCOTIA

She never wears another color. Black
Belonging to her is a brisk walk
Waking a field at night,
And on her way back something, a longing,
Breaks like a face beside her
In the store light.
Large white onions are pulled from serious
Poverty on the grocer's shelf, then dropped
Into the dark bottom of a paper bag. Ice crystals

Spiral on the windshield, clouds
Behind them made her jump
Like larkspur growing with Indian pipe deep inside
The hollow log. Grain sacks are
Doubled over in the back seat, a prospect
For the wind over this Christmas. She is thankful

For the ride
And watches the North Star through the edges
Of a hazel leaf pinned to the rubber blade
On the glass. She talks about
Her hair thin on her skull like cracks
Swimming over the vase in her kitchen window
Above the raw spinach
Draining in the day's dark sink.

SUN CALENDARS

The sink is filling with water
And the young girl remembers
Last winter, how snow would blow
Through the tigers of the lattice gate.
She and her grandfather danced
While the mirror's wavy face looked up
At the small oil painting of Bear Island.
She's just learned how to imagine what's left
In glass after so many reflections of light,
Her grandmother combing her hair
And the great migrations of bears across mountains,
Lakes, years.
        She will be shown
Photographs of her father's icehouse, door open
With a black stove inside. Her mother's first catch
Dangling from a line wrapped around her mitten
Above a dark circle of ice. She will figure
She's rich in seasons, her blood
A river old enough for sun to find
A sandy bank grown over now with pines.

VENA CAVA

The pane is clouded with my breath
Circling around my father's head
That sinks and rises, his shovel

Heaped with snow. The bank he's building
Will soon blot out my face. I'll learn
To breathe another way just as my eyes
Will sharpen, cut a precise line
Wide enough for my whole body
To slide through to the other side. I'm

Not going to turn back,
Making it this far, mid-way
Where it's quiet and suddenly warm:
I could lean my head against
The dark wall that fits me as well
As anything ever will and sleep,
But I have already offered myself
The light opening on the path
My father made. I'll follow him for awhile.
But after he kicks his second boot
Against the back of the stairs and
We have reached the door inside, I'll whisper
Goodbye and come running towards him

From the window where my grandmother sits,
All this time, reading aloud to me again
That story of the woman frozen to stone.

ON THE FOURTH DAY/AFTER
THE SECOND DISSOLUTION
OF STRINDBERG'S MIND

"There is something real behind
this play of inert matter . . ."
August Strindberg

I have found the two small hands
Of my son while following the grain
On a strip of bark. I back away from him,
The clasp of his fingers, white and raised
Toward heaven, complicated in prayer.
I am more son than father, more lost
Than he is in his ragged wood. But I am

Obsessed with the irregular
And let my eyes drift to a star
Of frost on the window: There, Napoleon
And his mistress riding bareback
Through the open doors
Of the cathedral at Chartres . . . I'm less

Than content — three pianos have been moved
Into the room next door and those old ladies
Are pounding nails in the walls. They
Would have me think that I am haunted

But it's this room
With its true acts of suddenness: the toothbrush
Dropping to the tiles and my curtain rods
Clanging down for no reason.
I am exhausted by my own trust —

Right here, at this very moment, I can see
In the peeling wallpapers, the antlered arms
Of my wife sparking velvet against a tree.
My son now beside her and I think

They'll turn towards me in my sleep,
Changed into boars by then,
Wild and gnawing,
Not one bone left unclean.

POSTPARTUM

The island bristled like a fist of spoons
In the sun. He came from there
In his mother's canoe, his red cap
Turned backwards
As if he were being pulled
In two directions. A visit

To the shore, to our house on Sundays
Was his mother's habit of casting
Herself over water, nibbling
At a fresh-baked pie and with my mother
Behind closed doors, speaking
As if her words were insects dragging
Their legs through pollen.
Once, through a breach in the door,

I heard him say: "Stay back,
Two heads in her stomach, knocking . . ."
Just a dream, my mother said
While twisting a braid in dough, and
You were the lucky one. The canal
Or the cord that choked your brother
After you was a chance
You've already taken,
A chance given.

The pipe railing with its dull glaze
Down the stairs to the landing
Was separated from one of its sockets —
When it bounced up in the air, he laughed
And started the dog barking. With a few turns
He'd have it right . . .

He untied the yellow rope
From around the swollen rib
Of the canoe, and loosened the knot
Around the birch, clumping it all
Into a ball and in a swirling arc,

He watched it darken into water.

ACTING OUT THE BODY

My first bathing suit with cups,
White with yellow rings
And a low back
Rounding off all of the knots
In my spine. I stood in a cove

Of mirrors as if watching the buoys
On a curved line, rising
Reflections that did not lie.
My breasts were round
And hidden, who knows how small
Or swollen — some boys

There beside the radio in the sand
Turning over on their backs
In unison. The sun goes down

And the saleswoman has ripped open
The cloth curtains, white magnolias
Under large pink hands almost
Make me cry. Naked,
I did not exist.

DEAD MAN'S FLOAT
For D.C.

The lake, I said, was too cold,
The waves, choppy enough
For it not to work. I stopped trying

To pretend I was your sister, murdered
You said, by a prisoner escaped from Attica,
No blood because I was strangled

With that dog's leash lying in the sand:
I saw your limbs, white as the cotton
On the inside of an orange skin, the whole of you

Swollen with air. You didn't need a story,
You said,
You had a flair . . . and still, you're in my sleep,

In my secret pond of the obsessed:
The head that bobs like a dark ball
Drifting toward the raft

I'm standing on. I wave to you
To stop, to wring the night
Out of your flesh, to watch

This morning: the beach raked clean.

SPEAKING OUT OF DOORS

Even with beacon lights
From the used car lot sweeping
The ball field, the dugout
Is a sanctuary for shadows, a hole
Unplugged and seeping
With the torso of a bat boy I once knew.
He didn't know it then but I watched

From behind the gray obelisk where the original
Owner of the park was buried
With his handsome horses and wife. With three
Lives to his name, pitcher, batter, catcher,
The boy played his game alone. There was
A real bat and ball but they lay like limb
And socket unhinged, belonging more
To the earth than to the flesh.
                                    When a fight

Broke out inside him, he settled it
With the only voice he knew — arms waving
Across the plate, *Safe,* he screamed
I didn't laugh out loud:
I remembered a bear I saw
Down from spring in the mountains,

Down to this same field in daylight,
Crazy and afraid, chasing
The boy's brother and all the while,
His lime sifter trailing behind him
In zig-zags. The grass stood up that day
The powder wound around the border trees,
The day he swore me to say, *Never,*
Holding my wrists to the ground, the obelisk
And dugout buckling under twilight.

THE CLEANING GIRLS

The host wasn't Body yet
But we imagined a communion
Taking place out of a shoe box
In the sacristy. For us, the broken wafers,
The imperfect ones from the factory were
Paper sails not to be entered
Into the celebration the very next morning, and
As the old priest had said,
These are for you
If you want them. Our work at the noon hour
Took us from the salt grass
To the quiet quarters near the reliquary

At the front of the church. We cleaned and replenished
The glass cruets with wine and water, not
Yet blood, not yet abundance,
But it stuck
To my fingers like blood
I had spilled from my own nose
Up and down the academy stairs. Maybe

We were intended
To take into ourselves, as sacrifice,
The unblessed, the discarded parts
That tasted like dry wind, that
With any faith would die down
To a whisper, a picture of Body

Rowing hard with one arm toward town.

LESSONS

A white-tailed deer crossed
In a burnt grass running along our thumbs.
My preoccupation with learning
The names of wildflowers
And birds, repetitions of first sight
Identical with each step forward, halted
Suddenly with the long, terrific gaze
Of the animal who might have been for the first time
Foraging without his mother. The face
Of a goldfinch enters along with my morning's
Idea to cut my hair, freshen the distance
It takes to walk from the kitchen to the table,
And then, in bed at night —
                              some cave-painted woman
With perfect strands of understanding
Leading off my dreams . . .
But I have given up the easy, girlish remedies
For acquiring the sense of something new,
Something on the verge of becoming, and the names,
Say, the yellow burrs of sticktight, I prize
Will have more to do with the water they drink,
With the steps we didn't take, taken from us,
Gladly.

SERMON ON THE LAKE

Runs of vine, up and down the walls
Of the stone church, brightened
Like catbrier after the squalls,
After all the boats had been swept
Off the lake. Only the birds

Returned to the calm white sky,
A jab of wingtip, a skirl
Of echoing points . . . The choir

Will be welcoming the new minister
This Sunday, shaking hands
After services and fanning the air
With sheet music, but there will be
One young girl running past them
Down the draft of stairs,
The thin neck of an iris flapping
Over the grip of her starched glove.
She will hurry to the edge

Of the stone landing, the flower
Resting in a white sock
Inside her black shoe . . . The sky points

Will keep her afloat while she dreams
She's the visible light in the bones
Of fish, the bread of angels.

HOUSE-SITTING IN NEW HAMPSHIRE

Barefoot behind the glass door,
I'm watching snow fall and slip
Into the black shoe of the lake. I do not
Expect any visitors tonight — have kept
The gate open all the same.
If the telephone should ring, it's here
Beside me in the middle of the unfinished
Picture frame. I can't decide which
It will be, the whaling boats or a woman
Walking the edge of a bluff, the grass overshot
With a burning sun. I hope something new
Will come, and with it, some morning
That opens only once and then,
Closes itself around me and I become
Its flesh, its acquired taste. The dryness

In the room, waterstained pans on the radiator
And the two cups holding the sag of the solitary
Afternoon tea; these, I think, are almost
Comforting, how the night can wrap you up
And how you don't try to scratch the blackness
Out of it, but wait with the patience of snow
Accumulating on the roof of the birdhouse,
The perfect triangle brightening
For the small bird in flight across water.

CLASSICISM ON THE WATER

He hasn't touched a drop in years
And thinks his whole life
Has been caught by a fierce
Belatedness — a dream, on the other hand,
That reels on without him
Ever catching up. As he stands
On the shore of the lake,
Squeezing our names between his hands,
More like birdcall
Than a real desire to join us,
I'm sure, this night, he'd understand
The intersection of lights across the sky
And in the water, our lives
Never belonging
Only to themselves — The way
Our rowboat angles, advancing for the idea.
I'm shaken by the eagerness
Already draining from his face
As he bends the boat down, climbing
Into the middle seat. He says, Why not
While we watch the radiant spin
Of the oars and stars. He suggests
A race to the island and back,
A panic-run for tomorrow
When each of us in our own boats
Would meet and gather at the landing.
I ask him if he's ever dreamed
The same dream twice but he says,
Impossible. My husband reminds him
Of the elements in dreams we share: a bird
Flying out of a linden into another, or

The birches we burn
In our separate houses, their smoke
Intercepting the moonlight in rooms
Far away and near as we are now
To scraping this boat against the sandy bottom.
He laughs and thinks we have it all
Confused, that truth is in watching
The scparateness of things, a snail
From a frog, and the distance
We're removcd or
Set back from fleshy progress.

II

WHITE HORIZON

IN DISTANCE

Slowly, you take a walk
In a northerly direction
Past the date palms and the low
Windows of adobe houses. Muffled

Music can be heard as ripe olives
Are crushed over stones. You
Remember how it was for your son
Who stumbled once, whose lungs collapsed
Along the runners' path. Through tall grass

You watch the rail and roadbed
Recede to the East as the road ends
With the stance of horses,
Six on them in regular stalls
Facing the whirl, rope and pole
Of their iron walker. Between the ranch

And the setting sun, your bodies
Flatten under the enormity of sky.
The hay, peach-brown and darkening,

Flies up
With an unexpected rearing . . .
The train whistle

Blows you back with no place left to go.

VOICES IN THE WATERJAR

I'm walking with the neighbor's boy
Up a hill to the open gate
Of an Indian cemetery.
                    Tall pines
Engrave the air, rinsed
By a three-day rain. Stones polished

With light tumble forward
Ahead of us to where the paths stop, worn grass
At every headstone. The boy hurries on

As if nothing could stop him, nothing
Marking his way but what loomed
Above his head at the far left corner,
A ragged kite like speckled wings . . .
                    He pulls out a coin
From his coat pocket and after holding it in the cup
Of his breath, quickly slides it
From behind his ear — a surprise
For the nearest grave
Already adorned with tiny statues of women
Whose cloth dresses bleed their colors
Into arms and legs, a dark blue straw.
            How clear the stalks are,
A few yellow goatsbeards
Crowding around a waterjar
Half-filled with rain. A prayer

Someone's telling, long and slow
Of cloud burials up on the one skin
With four poles.

LISTENING TO MOZART'S "JUPITER" NEAR THE DESERT AIRPORT

After the last concert on the radio
Until sleep, the arrival of a thousand birds
Just flown in for the winter,
For the overgrown grainfield cut
By the freshly oiled blades of a thresher. Silence

But for a starling who fills the emptiness
Between the pale shadows of the Joshua tree —
Like a black croquet ball
Passing through the dry wickets of air. An hour

More of this will follow, then drunken
Students dragging a rake
Through sand and over an anthill, laugh —
Night flights clamoring
In intervals, coathangers in the dark.

THE STITCH

Peeling the shells off a dozen boiled eggs,
I know
The life-bowl is filling too fast.

A breeze, sharp as any April
Coiling in my lungs, the jays
In the birdbath, bits of shell
Sticking to my forefinger and thumb,

My mother at the screen door,
Keys between her teeth,
Arms around a torn paper bag, plums
And tomatoes spilling to her feet.

She tells me to nevermind the fruit,
To sit at the table and listen,
To be quiet and look at her
Because something has happened, something

Serious, but my eyes
Are hooked to the whites of my knuckles
And the freeze of violet stitches,

The moment of flesh healing itself,
A boiled egg, blued
And the needle drawn

And the way back to where I withdraw
From my mother's news
Of an accident
That has killed
Two friends.

My mother collects the fruit.

She says it only happened
An hour ago.

She rinses the eggs to be chilled.

My shoulders shake.
She looks at the coffee tin
Brimming with lard.

Ovenbirds scold the rain out over the yard.

BUTLER POND

The wild ducks have taken first flight
Short dive and skid across
The water's surface like a fresh graze
Above the eye. Every feather
In its place, each wave
An unattenuated strum
Across pond-glow. Just moments before
They were nesting in their saucers
Of dry leaves behind the willowed walls
They would break through. It was so simple

To imagine these lives as safe
Warm bodies tucked under the appearance
Of shoreline. No one would have noticed
Had it not been for the man hunting weasel
In nearby scrub. The scent of musk
Followed by the *brub, brub* of a leather jacket
Against the branches of trees.

                           With one clean shot
The weasel dropped next to the abandoned
Nest. Its last breath a squeal
Almost like laughter, or was it
The hunter himself holding up
By its paws the dead animal. Its fur was red
Like the sun except for the white throat
And belly gliding downwards, last
Shudder before nightfall.

WITHIN EYESHOT

Taken up with photographs
His room was hung from the ceiling,
Cesnas, fighter planes, a goshawk
Bound in a red hood. A leather jess
Tightened around a black fist. The sky
Was too blue ever to be real, overexposed
And as thick as a wall painted over
By generations. But my brother would rivet
His stare for hours, only his narrow feet
Strained to curl like talons, would
Jitter against the air. Once, without turning
His eyes away from the ceiling, did he
Ask me, though he might have been
Talking to himself: Couldn't I
Just shake it off, the blind bird
On the ledge behind my eyes, let it
Fly off . . .
It was not all training I told him,
Someday we would be living in open places
Like Sante Fe or India, someplace
Where whatever it was, we'd see it
Right. We would love someone.
He groaned and left me standing there
Under all the stilled wings. Half-stunned,
I walked down the hallway and paused
Against the ladder let out of the opened trap
To the attic. Cold air rushed around me
And I retreated into my mother's call. At dinner
He stood and announced that he was leaving,
Veering out on his own, he said. He dropped down
In his chair and waited,
But his words fell with him
Like seed unswallowed into a father's hand.

AFTER THE SORREL DIED

A few broken stones rest against the door
Opening the pink adobe house. The child
Inside holds a doll
Between her legs on the worn carpet,
Neither of them are wearing clothes
But the dry, red peppers
She's tied together weight her neck
And abdomen. She is quiet

But we can hear her mother pulling weeds
In the garden, the heavy silence
Of a wheelbarrow about to be filled;
The shy witness of birds
Darting behind the leaves.

The Aunt is spinning
A silver wheel. Every sheet from the line
Is unpinned, then folded into squares
Like large bandages blocking out the sun.
Their beds will smell of oranges
The night the first fireflies
Come as bits of moon. A truck

With a squeeze-horn screwed to its door
Drives up under the old salt cedar. Dust
Swirls a band of sand flies
And red ants, dizzying
Like black curtains
Being drawn against a storm. A man
With large arms is hauling an angry goat
Over his shoulders. Its cloven hooves
Shine as they squeeze out
Of his hands, but he is kind
And sings the goat a song
About the sweet milk of her sisters
He's sipped in the shade.

WHITE HORIZON

When father decided to leave us
For the country of his birth,
I abandoned my life in the room
For a dark round of pines, sodden with snow.

I held my head back until my eyes opening on sky
Saw his head, low in his collar
Against the wind, turn a corner.

A dead traffic light swings forward
And back on a low wire at dusk
In the city. There is nothing to direct them
Through the intersection but his belief
In turning . . .

In an exchange into white I saw
His head rushing past the skyscraper's marble
Stairs and vanish into the shine
Of noise in the hotel's lobby. The large
Fireplace, and towels

Like cut lilies piling up against the tiles
And sink. His eyes, glistening
While he pinched tobacco into the damp
Fold of thin paper sheets. Smoke and dreams

To soften the darkness and cold. No grounds
And everywhere a clean streak of reality, white
Limbs above my head and a voice
Inside him that must have said: "It doesn't matter.

Life's a scattering of clouds
In everybody's sky. We'll polish the dark.

We are the kind with a dream
Of last night's fire and snow."

AT FIFTEEN

The parallel is exact, two sides
Of a nutshell, he said, with Moscow
In the field. These maples and birch
Are only camouflage . . . Great stores of water
In case of fire after blast-off. My father
Said to keep away the curious
Sunday drivers — Just there
Where the jay sits, right under
That rotting log is a silver hatch
That can be lifted. The stairs
Are deep and sink into the dark . . . The abandoned

SAC base with tunnels
Leading to rooms, dry cots
With pillows and green blankets
Stretched so tight a nickel could fly.
And it's still here
For us, for friends who have stumbled
Into a field, a site invisible
Even to the sky, between walls
In the earth.

OUR RIGHTFUL PLACE

On a cool sheet of linoleum stretched out
In your attic, I learned to lift the weight
Of your flesh, and with my heels, dug deep
Against the slanted roof
Where you had drawn in chalk a sun
I told you looked like an onion
Pulled out with its roots. The crooked
Light landed in my eyes and I could see
Ecstasy: A horse flying
Through a mountain pass, thistle and gorse
Growing out of rock
On either side. The room smelled of salt and
Camphor, pink garment bags on their rack
Like the long tongues of panting animals. A few
Watercolors hung in the rafters:
The old man and a clay pipe fading in a dizzy fringe
Of shadow. Endlessly, I can hear
The children playing down in the juniper,
One counting blind against a tree. . . .

WHILE WAITING FOR CHILDREN
for Hannah

We followed the flickering porch light
North through a field,
Our eyes opening to darkness
Slowly as the young ferns unravelling
By turns. It is a March evening
And we've just returned home
After a long meal in the woods.
The gray poplars there,
At dusk, all lean to the West. Now,

From behind our window
We watch a green lacewing
Fan its message in the stalling light,
A flittering of wings against the glass,
Against the shale-gray ears of the cat —
He knows nothing

Of the white silk cocoon that was
Her home, how it began:
                                  Eggs aloft —
The hardened gum stalks on the stem
Of a birch at the back of the field,
The spinneret of her mother
Weaving life's long day
For this. We will turn off the light
In an hour for sleep, all the children
Home by then, and after the whispers,
Wind.

FEUD

It's spring and the boys
Are popping their guns at the willows,
Cork and string stunning
The new buds like bees. The girls

Can see smoke inside the rain,
Black diamonds tumbling into their footsteps
In the mud. One of their mothers

Will have spilled her morning coffee,
The names of her husband, her son
Drowning in newsprint across the kitchen
Table. There is steam. She is sure
She can hear the pounding of blood
In her ears, blood spilt for money,
For a son against his father. The girls
Calling with their husbands, with food;

And that story of the catfish,
A cigar in its mouth, sitting on her pillow
Will never have to be heard again.

NIGHT TRAIN

The stars above the open boxcars
Might be fastened
To a load of coal and oranges . . .
I've tried not to think about your murder,
About those shots in the woods, lead
Tearing through your body, the car door open
And the light left on inside:

I dreamt of birds
Cracking through their shells —
You were climbing

That old pine of your childhood
And when you reached the top,
You cried. Your flesh wore every needle
You thought you left behind.
All of your brothers laughed,
Each of them calling to you
To climb down before it rained.

You saw lightning over the pond
And quilled dust rising over the humped shoal
Of the baseball diamond. Like a crib tossed on hot coals,
The room I wake to rattles by.

MIDSUMMER SUNDAY

Tossing pieces of bread to the birds
Collecting on the grassy tiers
Down to the lake, I saw you

Lying face down in the hammock,
A towel draped over your naked back
And sides to the ground. I crawled
Under with a pair of scissors,
Cutting one diamond of air
From another. You fell through the net

Just when the fireboat passed
The dock — fish scattering
In all directions, a strand

Of my hair snagged in your teeth,
Your eye pressed against mine, a wedge
With a spur of light between.

THE MAINTENANCE MAN AND THE MODEL

He's sitting in a canvas chair,
His balls hanging out
Of his torn shorts, rings of smoke
Blowing around the words
He's picked up from the philosophy student
In unit ten: tertium organum, élan vital, and
Reincarnation. She listens and takes

A dive down to the bottom of the pool,
Wrestles with the weight of his ideas
Pressing down now on her body
So hard something is bound
To give . . . surfacing,
She doesn't understand
The clench in her chest, doesn't want
To feel anything for a man
With a few words, torn shorts,
And a body he can't control. She lifts herself

Out of the water, slings her towel
Over her arm and walks away. She hates
This man for making her feel sorry,
She hates the key she dropped
Before opening the door and the breasts
That threaten release
As she bends. She never wants

To live this life all over again.

ANGRY AT NO ONE

He's not himself today. He won't shower
Inside the cabin but has
Taken a cake of marbled soap
Down to the stream where
There are no neighbors to watch him
Strip, and beginning with his chest,
Scrub the daylights out of his skin

Until there, in the cottonwood shadows,
Stands an abominable man, bristling
Like an isolationist coming to terms
With the fact of his own existence. *One*
For sorrow, two for mirth . . . pausing
At the genitals, he notices a white streak
Down the black wing of a magpie
Shoot across the water. The bird lands
And stares from the burnt-out jaw
Of a stump, just long enough
For him to mirror even the cry,
Head-high above the cold iron hooks
Of the stream. The bird has joined his assembly

Far inside the woods. The man, rubbing
His torn foot and body dry, flicks next
His head and dresses with a calm

You'd think, stolen from the sky.

THREE LANDSCAPES

After Hiroshige

I. THE TRAVELERS

Their lives are carried
In baskets over a river
By lines of heavy rope their friends have made —
Hemp and animal hair
Twist through the late afternoon
Gorge like the tortured clouds
That stretch behind the mountain.
Trees spindle at cross-angles
From the over-hanging cliffs. The tuning
Of the pipe is for the pleasure
Of the water snake. The travelers
Balance themselves with their slippers,
A satin cushion in each pocket. Before the downward
Wind passes through the blond thatching
In the floor of the basket, it circles
Their blue-capped heads
And works around their lotus
Like the whorling of lichen on the watermarks
Against the glutted space below them. It is
A spectacle of labor and ease, the tug and slide
Of lives they will join — from the middle
That is the river's unweighted moment,
An almost clearing air.

II. THE GRANDMOTHER'S CURE

Every house will have its flowers
And the grandmothers will cross over to the iris bank
Of the river. All winter there has been sickness

But now it is April and Grandfather
Is waiting for the warm poultice
To heal his sores. The women will fade through
The tall grasses to the edge of the water
Where the iris grows, leaving behind them
The sunset, the roofs of their houses cast together
Like the black glass scales of a dragon. The tall flowers

Will be cut and carried back in the dark,
Laid out on mats to dry
In the weekday sun. Stems and petals
Crushed into a fine blue powder will release
The last of winter from within the blistered skin
And from the corners of the snow-blind eyes,
Tears of patience. Abandoned,

The remaining irises stand in the foreground
Like the punishment towers
Of the Imperial nunnery.

III. Birth

The waterfall swayed a little past the window
When the doctor entered the quiet room.
She and her husband forgot
Their premonitions of a broken-down footbridge
Across the river and the barges dragging
Their visitor below, a violet gash
On the water's back. She was sure of only one thing,
The silver instruments sinking out of the black bag
Strangled by weeds. In their hours of waiting

They watched the cherry trees on the hill
Blossom into damask vapors
Under the limbs of their companions,
The black pines. Her labor was long,

Each pain coiled around the gentle words
That sprung in the room like the Aron lily
And the bulrush, a reminder
From the flower master who told them
To carry 'Nothing' in the heart. But nothing

Could keep them from the last long moment
Breaking itself open with joy, the first cries
Of their son like the staggering flight of a crane
Climbing the face of the waterfall.

III

IN THE OPEN AIR

SHADOW AS AN ARTICLE OF FAITH

The rosewood crucifix at the end of the hall
Among the plum flowers of the wallpaper
Is half-lit from the bare arms
Down to the scrubbed shadows
Of the floor. A missing tile, breaking the concentration

Of the young novitiate, shares the sun's influence
Around his black gown
Like the large thrush that morning that fell
Out of his dream onto the pillow. He would not
Be trapped like this

For the claim he's made
On the hour; it was all a simple matter of a tile,
Something he would report
At dinner. It is not like the hospital,

The heart attack who looks at him
As if he were the one with steel shoes
Kicking through the gray walls
Above Los Angeles. No. Here it is one
Devotion. One heart that follows
The hour and the white rope
Along the outside wall near the highway

Where the bridge that collapsed in the earthquake
Is a blue steel hexapod thrown on its side,
Its spurs tearing out
All the light from the sky.

SUMMER MONSOON

They stood on the balcony in their undershirts
While the wind shook the palm
Forward and back like the head of a witch doctor.
The dates inside their yellow husks
Swung through the torn air and
He cupped her breasts for a coolness of flesh
He'll remember smelling like egg whites and lime.

Bumping their heads against the wild fern
And asparagus hanging from the ceiling,
They watched the pink and orange glow holding on
In the streetlights, the spider in a wax grip
Tearing up the floor of a candle. They huddled
Under a faded blanket he'd dug out
From a trunk in the cellar. She saw

In there once, the medals, jacket, boots,
Photographs of Asian women and children
Without shirts and their tags swinging
Low over the skin-tightness
Stretched between their nipples. . . .

Once, and he'd never let her look again.
But still she'll remember his eyes, the boy
In the photo who stares at her with shadows
Spotting his face like the back of an Inca dove

Swaying on a branch in rain.

SNOW WATER COVE

Under the graying windows, the brook
Dams quickly
With a few stiff branches like the grappling paws
Of a timber wolf.
The steps and pine railing glazed with ice
Shoot down from a torn screen door.

Above me rusted bear traps
Hang from the porch ceiling
                     and sway
As they grit the air.
                The table is piled with poles
And a braided straw tackle box. Among the ordinary
Hooks and flies, a lead sinker
The size of an egg wells up
From under the breastbone and feathers
Of a hawk; the cat takes a sniff
And returns to chasing the light
Thrown by a silver lure. Inside the open cupboard

Small dishes of poison
And an alabaster hand offering
A cube of resin. The blond violin resting
In the glass case shines as no other, a face

In wintertime lifting off a stretcher.

BURIAL

Under the heavy boughs of the spruce
Where the snow is left untouched,
One small blotch of sun
Like the flooding wires
Of the empty rabbit cage
Comes to hold you. As if inside
A blue bottle, you're remembering
How spring watched you gather
In your torn gloves those unruly wings
And the small throbbing body
Of the sparrow after it struck
The kitchen window. The whole body
Stiffened and the pads of your fingers
Burned and shook like the flexing
Blade of the neighbor's handsaw
As he whipped it over his head
Until it sang in the air
Above the birch he was stacking
For the last storm of the season.

THE BLUE DONKEY

The idiot boy with one glass eye
Spit his entire stock of words into the dark
Mouth of the river — a favorite vow
Taken every year before his pilgrimage
To the chapel of the virgin
Who talked to him from her half-shell
In the side of the mountain. She told him

To go back to the river, drink
From his hands and return to her
In continued silence. When he had done this,

He would take out the round glass
From its orbit, place it in her open palm
And wait there beside her
Until he heard the bell of his donkey
Ringing for him at the river's bend; then

His eye was his again and he could go back
To the village where everyone for the first time
In all their lives, would understand him . . .

There was great celebration, flags streaming,
Tambourines, and pointed paper hats
Floating on the heads of all who welcomed him.

His donkey stood beside the fountain.
It began to kick and bray,
Telling the boy, idiot or not,
He loved him, and he loved the world better
Since every inch of him was blue,
Blue as glass against the white wilderness
Of the opened hand.

SPRING THAW

The lake's thaw is a man's sleep,
A body of sleep that will wake
With a wooden spoon in its mouth.
The oar stuck in the sandy rift
Is about to fall and float back
Between an island and a pole house.

The moon hurries through all of its phases
As I stand on the shore holding the hand
Of someone who feels like an ancestor.
We are without faces here. We are the stars
We look at. The paper of winter is now
The hydrangea spinning through the dark.

The road spirals off over mountains,
A conversion of steps and April
Coming on out of long storms. The dream
Nearing its end, the softness of ferns:

We reach the session of rocks like shelves
Our bodies warm to. It is love's hands
Under an open sky, a clear sounding.

SEPARATE GIFTS

I.

I let my body drop down
From inside itself into the grass.
In a corner of the yard
My grandmother prods and rakes
The morning's egg shells into the dark swell
Of the compost heap, her necklace
Swinging to her time, her arms
Waving back the digger wasp
She maddened in the sun.

II.

All of the shades in the white room
Are drawn. I'm sinking straws
Into jars of spring water and lime.
We sit without words, our backs against
The cool mahogany, our breath taken
Slowly, sipping in the half-dark.

III.

The blankets smell of cedar
And ground pepper. I sleep
In the sewing room, "black bob-o-link"
Mounted on his table without a song
Or a dream I can't wake from. She sleeps
Beside a strict order of combs,
But there is a streak of the girl left
In her footprints in powder
Lifting off a naked floor.

IV.

The pipes in the closet are steaming.
Shoes, coats, dresses
Scattered on the stairs. Trucks have come
To empty her house, strangers
With heavy arms and folding faces —

Chairs and tables with my name
Chalked under them,
Lifting above a spray of coal ash
Out on the icy sidewalk. Our field
Closing its wings under the skyline.

THE ROOMER

It began with a fishing net
Stretched across the window, then
Those stairs, long ago walled in
And leading up to the room
For salesmen
Needing a place to sleep . . .

                    Plaster and
Sunlight breaking inside my sleep, your voice
Calling down, asking that someone
Take the stones
You struck together in your hands, a study

Of storms passing over.

I wanted to ask
How it was that the dead have hands,
And if I touched them, would I
Be changed? I saw a sea horse

Feeding on the grasses of the estuary,
Its body growing under the quick pivot
Of its eyes; your hand
Smoothing down the jagged mane . . .

A child's hand dips into a glass gallon jar,
Hundreds of sea horses, caught and dried,
Yellow and lacquer, all down the coast.

The coastline recedes and the dead
Geraniums along the saltbox porches
Rock in their wicker baskets.

It is a December
Afternoon, my hands
Sunk deep into my pockets, alone

With what my mind has made . . .

[57]

IN THE OPEN AIR

In the corner of the sunroom was a bowl
    Full of possibility,
Carved by a Portuguese artisan and wine
Seller who had in mind a summer evening
After it rained and the lawn had been cut,
Loose grass stuck to us,
Slippery as the glass of milk pulled across
The blue and white oilcloth. It was
    A mineral landscape through which a long
Fingernail drags its jagged ridge:
A mountain rises above the mist
And the butter leaves and radishes in the swoop
    Of the bowl are felt to be "The moment from
Here on out," the conversion of matter like this
Into time or say, clicking your fingers
To confuse the hens, kernels of corn extinguished
    Into thin air . . . Pretty soon, we'll see
Replication, embroidering in our chairs
After the sun's gone down: a fruitfly introduces itself,
Its midget inscriptions, and even the dander
    On the would-be stems and cucumber
In that bowl, I see it now, its time over
    And it's that way, the shelf,
Life's order.

FOR THE UNCLES

The shore is abandoned and her friends
Are sleeping beside a basket of fruit
That's wrapped in blue cellophane. The manager
Of the Alhambra Hotel has provided at least
One gift for his three only guests — pity
For them for looking so small, out of place
And unencouraged by the church.
It is Christmas Day in Málaga
And not one of them has understood
Why they travel to sleep
In strange beds, why
She dreams of a king snake
Coiled around a lighted candle
That's sunk in a mound of flour
In someone's larder. And then,
An elderly couple arguing over how much coal
To shovel into the fire. The young archeologists
Are roasting a pig today,
Tomorrow they will turn their faces
Toward the sun. They'll all say they swam
In the Mediterranean because it's part
Of a story, something the families will expect
Around New Year's. After supper, they will be
Driving across the Hudson and the falls
Will be frozen, white horses climbing,
She'll lean over to her uncles
And say, the sea, the Mediterranean,
It's like God, another matter.

MONOTONY
— circa 1946

Drying knives at the window
She's doing what she's been told:

Set the turkish towel
In your palm, let
                the corners fall
Like Mayweed, don't smudge
The silver by touching it
                at all . . .

While he's in St. Louis, she watches
The gray squirrel on the line
Between two poles, back and forth —
A monotony, a geography
And an appetite like her husband's
If he returns
To his kitchen in Topeka.

The other woman, without a name,
Has the bridge, the Missouri
And the gardens to keep him,
But that wouldn't be enough. He'd say
There must be more. Give me rain,
The drizzle and a few dreary Sundays
Beside a porcelain stove. Yes,
And his skin must be steaming,

Sliding him down in her chair. Then,
His wife's face
Blown-up in smoke, the color
Of squirrel spanning the edge of a mountain.

HOLDING IN SUMMER

The front porch sags,
Wind and gravel cross the low tin roof
Like the beaded expeditions of prayer
For her father who was a soldier
In France. She can feel him beside her
When miles of lake pull up
From both ends by a bow of strawlight
As she hums. They all fall back
Into a long stall of cool air
Near the varnished wall
Her grandmother breaks behind.

The wind is made from inside the shore,
Her line of fears —

Water labors through walls
Like her legs divining over
The thick carpet. Elephants
In red and gold fields follow
Birds inside the tasseled border. She is called
With the promise she made
                              not to cry
For her father.

Flannel and fog curl into drawn sheets.
She is kissed so quickly
Doorlight and slippers sweep down
The stairs. Through the grilled vents
In the floor, she can hear
How the cards snap
At the wooden table.
Over and over, bone and grain —
Solitary wishes
To drown out bells and drifting stars.

The summerhouse sleeps on a gray head of fog.

SHADOW OF THE OX

Clouds steamed above the still tractor
While the black tongue of an ox
Wrapped itself around the petals
Of pink campion. . . . I awoke
To the drowse of musty violets,

To the neighbor's blind baby
Playing spoons on her mother's roasting pan —
We were lost everytime she missed,
Everytime the dog barked. I thought
I saw the man I love
Standing beside the ox, a light
Breeze between them, then shadow
Swirling above their heads like fish,
Fins locked.
                    Boys on a riverbank
Have tangled their lines and will be hours
Haggling over their catch. Vines
Waved out of their depths
As though they were the dead entering

The afterlife. Music as it is heard
In the second waking is large
Like the world, wind in strings
And the arrangement of memories
Drifting backward, sea-weary
Out of time.
Sunfish clipped from the line, light

Along a corridor of silver birches
And the ox grazing in an autumn
That is all seasons unknown to grief.

ACKNOWLEDGMENTS

The American Poetry Review: "Feud," "October Nights," "Six O'Clock in Nova Scotia," "Burial," "The Florist's Widow," "Listening to Mozart's 'Jupiter' Near the Desert Airport," "Snow Water Cove" (appeared under the title: "The Inheritance,") "Postpartum," "Shadow of the Ox," "The Maintenance Man and the Model," "The Cleaning Girls," "Speaking Out of Doors," "Angry at No One," "The Roomer"

The Bennington Review: "The Birth of the Mortician's Goddaughter"

The Glens Falls Review: "At Fifteen" (appeared under the title: "Walking with a Boy at Thirteen," "Acting Out the Body"

Hayden's Ferry Review: "Classicism on the Water"

The North American Review: "Within Eyeshot," "On the Fourth Day/ After the Second Dissolution of Strindberg's Mind"

Poetry Northwest: "The Blue Donkey"

Quarterly West: "A Milltown in Late Autumn," "For the Uncles," "House-Sitting in New Hampshire"

Telescope: "Shadow as an Article of Faith"